Canada's Birds

Susan Hughes

Scholastic Canada Ltd.

Toronto New York London Auckland Sydney
Mexico City New Delhi Hong Kong Buenos Aires

Photo credits:

Cover (downy woodpecker) © Shutterstock; (ruby-throated hummingbird) © Shutterstock; great horned owl © istock.com; Back cover © istock.com ; Page iv (all images) © istock.com; Pages 2, 3, 4 © Shutterstock; Page 6 © Tom Massung; Page 7 © istock.com; Page 9 © Richard Casterline; Page 10 © Fotosearch; Page 12, 15 © Shutterstock; Page 16 © Dr. George K. Peck; Page 17 © First Light; Page 19, 20 © istock.com; Page 22 © Shutterstock.com; Page 25 © istock.com; Page 26 © Fotosearch; Page 27 © Shutterstock; Page 28, 29 © Steve Shinn; Page 31 © Jan Smit/Foto Natura/Minden Pictures; Page 32, 34, 36, 37 © Shutterstock; Page 38 © Michael Quinton/Minden Pictures; Page 39 © Fotosearch; Page 40 © Robert Costello, Smithsonian's National Museum of Natural History; Page 41 (grouse on snow) © Shutterstock; Page 41 (grouse print in snow) © Bob McElroy; Page 44 © Fotosearch; Page 46 © E. R. Degginger / Photo Researchers, Inc.; Page 47 © Shutterstock; Page 48 © Keith Williams; Page 50 © istock.com; Page 52 © Michael Quinton/Minden Pictures

Library and Archives Canada Cataloguing in Publication

Hughes, Susan, 1960-
          Canada's birds / Susan Hughes.

(Canada close up)
ISBN 978-1-4431-0001-4

          1. Birds--Canada--Juvenile literature. I. Title. II. Series: Canada close up (Toronto, Ont.)

QL685.H78 2010   j598.0971   C2010-900169-9

Text copyright © 2010 by Susan Hughes.
All rights reserved.

No part of this publication may be reproduced or stored in a retrieval system, or transmitted in any form or by any means, electronic, mechanical, recording, or otherwise, without written permission of the publisher, Scholastic Canada Ltd., 604 King Street West, Toronto, Ontario M5V 1E1, Canada. In the case of photocopying or other reprographic copying, a licence must be obtained from Access Copyright (Canadian Copyright Licensing Agency), 1 Yonge Street, Suite 800, Toronto, Ontario M5E 1E5 (1-800-893-5777).

6 5 4 3 2 1   Printed in Canada   119   10 11 12 13

Table of Contents

Hundreds of Species 1

1. Black-capped Chickadee 2

2. Great Horned Owl 7

3. Downy Woodpecker 12

4. Killdeer 17

5. Ruby-throated Hummingbird 22

6. Northern Shoveler 27

7. Osprey 32

8. Ruffed Grouse 37

9. Yellow Warbler 42

10. Raven 47

Hundreds of Species

Canada is one of the biggest countries in the world. Across our land you can find wetlands, mountains, prairies, woodlands, coasts and tundra. There is hot weather and cold weather. There is sun, rain and snow.

This means that Canada has a range of habitats, and many kinds of birds can live here. Some live here all year round. Some fly south in winter. You may see certain birds only in certain parts of the country. Others you may see in many parts of the country. But altogether over four hundred species of birds call Canada home.

Come along and meet some of them!

Chapter 1

Black-capped Chickadee

Listen closely. Sometimes you can hear the call of this tiny bird before you spot it.

Chick-a-dee-dee-dee!
Chick-a-dee-dee-dee!

This call gives the little black and white fellow its name: chickadee. It uses this call, and many others, to communicate with nearby chickadees. It might scold an intruder. It might tell other chickadees where a predator is!

Chickadees flit about in small groups throughout Canada's forests. As they fly, they call softly to keep track of one another.

Maybe you've seen chickadees in an orchard, at your backyard feeder or even in a city park. Brave ones may even try to sneak seeds from the hand of a patient bird lover!

The chickadee mainly eats insects and their eggs. In fact, a chickadee is one of the forest's best pest controllers. It searches for insects and spiders along tree branches, tree trunks and even on pine needles. A chickadee also eats seeds, snails and fruit.

When there is lots of food, such as in the late summer or fall, the chickadee hides what it cannot eat. It sometimes hides as many as one hundred bits of food a day. The chickadee also has an amazing memory. It can remember where it stashed its food for up to twenty-eight days! This helps in the winter, when it's cold and food is hard to find.

On cold nights, chickadees can fluff up their feathers to stay warm. The thick feathers trap a layer of warm air next to the birds' little bodies.

In the springtime, chickadee flocks break up into mating pairs. Together the male and female dig a hole in the dead part of a tree or in a tree stump.

The female chickadee lays six to eight eggs. The eggs hatch in about two weeks. Both parents care for the babies. They bring them food and carry away the droppings. The mother keeps the babies warm until their feathers grow in.

After about sixteen days, the young chickadees are ready to leave the nest. Their parents may keep feeding them for two or three more weeks. But then off they go to join a new flock!

Chapter 2

Great Horned Owl

What is the first thing you notice about this owl? Is it its horns?

Despite the owl's name, what you see sticking up from its head are not horns. And no, they are not ears, either! The ears are slits on each side of the owl's head.

The "horns" are actually tufts of feathers. No one knows for sure what their purpose is. Maybe the owl uses them to communicate: tufts flat when it's relaxed, and tufts up when it senses danger.

The great horned owl can be found throughout Canada, except in the very far north. It is one of the most common large birds of prey in this country. How large is it? More than one metre from wing tip to wing tip — about the length of a kid's hockey stick.

The great horned owl stays in its territory. It hunts through the same part of the forest all year round. It preys on animals small and large — from other birds, mice, squirrels, shrews, snakes and frogs to gophers, rabbits and porcupines. It is one of the few creatures that will hunt skunks!

The owl cannot move its big yellow eyes. It must turn its entire head to look about. But that does not stop it from being a great hunter. It has excellent night vision and hearing. Soft feathers with fringes help the owl stay silent as it swoops down on its prey.

See the owl, perched on a branch? It spies its prey. Silently, swiftly, it swoops down on folded wings . . . There! The owl grabs its prey using the sharp claws on its feet called talons. This is why it is known as a "perch and pounce" hunter.

When it eats, the owl swallows small prey whole. It picks apart larger prey with its talons. But the owl can't digest everything it eats.

What happens to the fur, feathers, teeth and bones in its stomach? The owl's stomach squishes everything it cannot digest into a pellet, sort of like a garbage truck does with trash. The owl throws up the pellet later. Finding one of these pellets in the woods is a great way for scientists to learn about the owl's diet!

And babies? While the snow is still falling, the female great horned owl lays two or three eggs in her nest. After about a month, the eggs hatch. Now the adults must feed their hungry young. When the little ones are about five weeks old, they are about as large as their parents. They will soon leave the nest, sometimes before they can even fly!

Chapter 3

Downy Woodpecker

Of the thirteen kinds of woodpeckers that live in Canada, the downy woodpecker is the smallest. It is about the length of a pen. The male and female look a lot alike. But if you see a red bar on the back of the downy's head, it's a male.

The downy woodpecker eats berries, acorns and grains. But mostly it feeds on small insects and insect eggs. Sometimes they're easy to find. Sometimes the bird has to hunt for them! It searches in the cracks of tree trunks, branches or twigs.

The downy woodpecker is built for digging insects out of wood. Its bill is shaped like a chisel. Its tongue is very long and has barbs on it. It is also covered with a gluey substance. Insects and insect eggs stick to it!

The downy's nostrils are at the top of its bill. They are covered with feathers so bits of flying bark or wood powder can't get in.

The woodpecker has strong feet that help it cling to the bark as it drills. Its stiff tail feathers help to prop the bird up against the tree trunk.

Most large woodpeckers are too heavy to perch on the small branches of treetops. Not the downy woodpecker. It is small enough to feed on these thin branches. The males usually eat up here in the winter while chasing other birds away.

In fact, downy woodpeckers are so small they can search for insects on the branches of shrubs and bushes. They can even balance on thin goldenrod or corn stalks as they hunt!

There are other reasons it's good to be small. Because its bill is so tiny, the downy woodpecker can drill holes in the narrowest trunks of dead trees. It can make its nests where other, larger woodpeckers cannot.

It can take two to three weeks for a male and female to dig out a nest hole in a dead tree. Then they line the nest with wood chips. The female usually lays four or five eggs. The parents take turns sitting on the nest — the male usually takes the night shift!

About twelve days later, the young birds hatch. In three weeks they are so big that their parents are feeding them every three or four minutes! Soon the parents cut back on the meals. It's time for the young birds to head out in search of their own food.

Chapter 4

Killdeer

Look at that pretty bird with the black stripes. It's about the same size as a robin but it has longer legs. Oh, no, it is limping slowly along the shore, dragging its wing and calling. Is the bird's wing broken?

No it's not. The killdeer is playing a clever trick. It's pretending that it is easy prey. It is trying to lure predators, or curious humans, away from its nest of baby birds.

The killdeer is a shorebird — with a difference. It can live near water, but it is also found far from the water's edge.

When the killdeer nests, it just needs a flat space with short grass or pebbles and a clear view. This means killdeers nest across most of southern Canada in the summer — on beaches, in fields, at airports, on golf courses, along roads, even in parking lots.

It does not even really make a nest. The killdeer lays its four eggs in a hollow in the ground, which may be lined with some grass.

The pear-shaped eggs are a light yellow-brown colour with some dark markings. This makes it hard to see them against the earth or pebbles.

The killdeer puts the eggs in a circle with the pointy ends facing inwards. Why? Maybe they fit underneath the bird better when it sits on them. Maybe because the rounded ends have more markings, they are better disguised.

Both parents take turns keeping the eggs warm. They are also careful not to let the eggs get too hot. Sometimes a killdeer will stand over the eggs. The bird's body shades the eggs and lets the breeze cool them as well.

Baby killdeer are born with their eyes open. They are ready for action! They are covered in wet down, but it dries quickly. Young killdeer can feed themselves within one day. They run about on their long legs, pecking at insects. Killdeer like to eat grasshoppers, earthworms, beetles and snails.

Still, for many weeks, killdeer parents stand watch over their young. If there is danger, the parents give a loud alarm call and the babies freeze. A soft call tells the young birds to come and snuggle under a parent to sleep.

After forty days, the young birds can fly, and off they go, on their own.

Chapter 5

Ruby-throated Hummingbird

The ruby-throated is the most common hummingbird in Canada. In the summer months, it is found in the Atlantic provinces, Quebec, Ontario, Manitoba, Saskatchewan and Alberta.

Hummingbirds are truly amazing birds. They are the only birds that can hover in place in the air. They can even fly upside down!

A ruby-throated hummingbird will beat its wings over fifty times a second. The wings are attached to its body with a special ball-and-socket joint. This joint is only found in hummingbirds and swifts. It lets the hummers fly backwards and hover.

For its size, the hummingbird has the largest heart of any animal. Even when it is resting, the heart of the ruby-throated hummingbird beats about 250 times each minute! That's a lot — your heart only beats about 70–110 times a minute.

Ruby-throated hummingbirds migrate south to Central America every fall. They cross the Gulf of Mexico, travelling about 800 kilometres over the sea. In the spring, they fly north again.

Ruby-throated hummingbirds are tiny. The females are a bit larger than the males, but they still only weigh about as much as a nickel. They are so active, they need to eat a lot — one or two times their body weight in food every day.

They eat small insects and nectar from flowers. They do not sip or suck the nectar. Their long tongues are split at the end and the tips are brushy. They lap up the nectar, much as a cat laps milk. They stick out their tongues and snap them back up to ten times per second!

After mating, the female builds a nest. She collects the sticky silk of spider webs. She winds it around a branch, then attaches bits of plants. She covers the outside with lichen (like-en). Inside, she places plant fuzz. Her cup-like nest is the size of a walnut.

The female hummingbird lays two white eggs, each the size of a pea. The babies hatch in sixteen to eighteen days. They are naked and tiny, the size of honeybees.

The mother hummer loses weight while she busily cares for her babies. She is raising them all alone! She goes in search of nectar and insect eggs. When she returns, she squirts the food into her babies' mouths.

The baby hummingbirds grow feathers and get bigger. When the young hummers are about three weeks old, they leave the nest. They are now heavier than their over-worked mother!

Chapter 6

Northern Shoveler

Take one look at this duck and you'll know how it got the name shoveler. It has a huge bill that is shaped like a shovel or a spoon. Spoonbill is this bird's nickname. Its bill is longer than its head. It is over 3 centimetres wide at the tip!

The northern shoveler eats in an unusual way. Many ducks have something called lamellae (la-mel-lee) on the back edges of their bills. Picture the teeth on a comb — that's what lamellae are like.

Ducks use lamellae like a strainer. With their heads down, they swim through muddy water. Water comes in through the tips of the bills. When the water goes out through the lamellae, bits of food are caught in the bill and can be eaten.

The northern shoveler's bill has over one hundred lamellae that are very fine. This means even tiny aquatic animals, shellfish and bits of plankton remain in its bill. So northern shovelers can eat small bits of food that other ducks cannot.

Sometimes a northern shoveler will swirl in a circle while it feeds. Sometimes it seems to work with other shovelers in a group. They go through the water together, stirring up the mud from the bottom. Then they skim through it, searching for food. They look like a pinwheel!

You can find the northern shoveler across most of western Canada, especially in the prairies. It likes to live in wetlands, ponds and marshes. In the fall, it migrates to Mexico for the winter.

Northern shovelers return to Canada in the spring. A male and a female will choose a territory. The male northern shoveler fiercely defends his territory against all comers! When he sees an intruder, he gives a low quack. He pumps his head up and down, up and down.

The female builds a nest on the ground, near water. She scratches out a hollow and lines it with plants, feathers and down. She lays eight to twelve eggs. The ducklings hatch in about twenty-two days.

On the same day that the babies are born, the mother duck leads them away from the nest and into the water. Right away, they know how to swim! The mother cares for her ducklings for six to eight weeks. During this time, they grow and their bills change shape, becoming shovel-like. Then it's time to set off on their own!

Chapter 7

Osprey

Look at this magnificent bird. Is it an eagle?

It has a body like an eagle. It is also a raptor, like an eagle. But this bird is actually an osprey.

Ospreys can be found on ocean coasts, lakeshores and along rivers. They live on every continent except Antarctica. About one-third of all ospreys live in Canada. They migrate south in the winter.

What makes an osprey different from other raptors is its long, narrow wings. When it flies, the wings are bent on an angle. It also has four equal toes, unlike other raptors. The outer toe can bend forward or back. The osprey uses two toes forward and two toes back to grip its prey. Each toe has a long, curved talon. On the soles of the osprey's feet are short, hard spikes. The talons and spikes help it cling to its prey.

This is handy, because the osprey mainly eats fish. Imagine how slippery a wiggly, wet fish must be!

How does the osprey hunt? It looks for a slow-swimming fish. When it spots one, it hovers until the fish is in just the right spot. Then it dives down, feet first! Sometimes the osprey goes right under the water. It closes its nostrils so water can't get in, and it disappears in a huge splash!

Suddenly, there is the hunter again, holding the fish in its claws.

Often the osprey will fly to a nearby tree to eat. It will hold down the fish with one claw. It will pull the fish into pieces with its beak. It always eats the head first.

If a male osprey has a nest, it will return there with the fish. The nest is big and heavy and near water. It is made of large sticks. Sometimes, though, ospreys use trash — hula hoops, dolls and toy boats have been found in osprey nests.

In the nest a mother osprey waits with two or three chicks. Each chick needs to eat about 1 kilogram of fish a day!

Their parents take good care of them. They grow and grow. Their wings get very large! Their wingspan is around 1.6 metres — longer than a broom.

The chicks practise lifting and flapping their wings. The parents show them how to fly.

When the chicks are between one and two months old, they make their first flight from the nest. For another ten to twenty days they stay close to their parents. They may beg for food. Then one day, they lift their wings and take off. They are old enough to be on their own now.

Chapter 8

Ruffed Grouse

Put, put, put, put, purrrr...

Have you ever heard a bird make that noise? It sounds a little like an engine starting up. But it is actually a male ruffed grouse.

37

The grouse is cupping its wings and beating them against the air. This is called drumming. The sound warns away other males. In the spring, it also attracts females.

The male sits on a drumming post, such as a log or rock, near the edge of the forest. When he sees a female, his neck feathers spread out around his head, like an umbrella or ruff. He nods his head and spreads his tail. He struts.

After the male and female mate, they separate. The male remains in his territory. It has the food and shelter he needs.

The female chooses a place to make a nest. She lays seven to twelve eggs. When the babies hatch, she cares for them. Grouse like to eat leaves, buds, twigs, fruit and sometimes insects. To feed her babies, a mother may cross over the territories of a few males.

Her young can fly a short distance before they are two weeks old. By fall, they are almost completely grown. The young grouse move off on their own, trying to find a place to live in the forest. Now, the males drum again to mark their territory. No youngsters allowed! They'll have to find a territory of their own.

Soon it is winter. Ruffed grouse do not migrate. They are well adapted to spend the winter in Canada. They grow fringes or bristles on the sides of their toes. These act like snowshoes to help the birds travel over the deep snow.

Bristles on the grouse's foot.

They may also burrow into the deep snow. This keeps them warm. It also keeps them hidden from predators.

If you're ever walking in the forest in winter, you may be startled by a ruffed grouse. They've been known to come bursting out of the snow, surprising whoever is walking by!

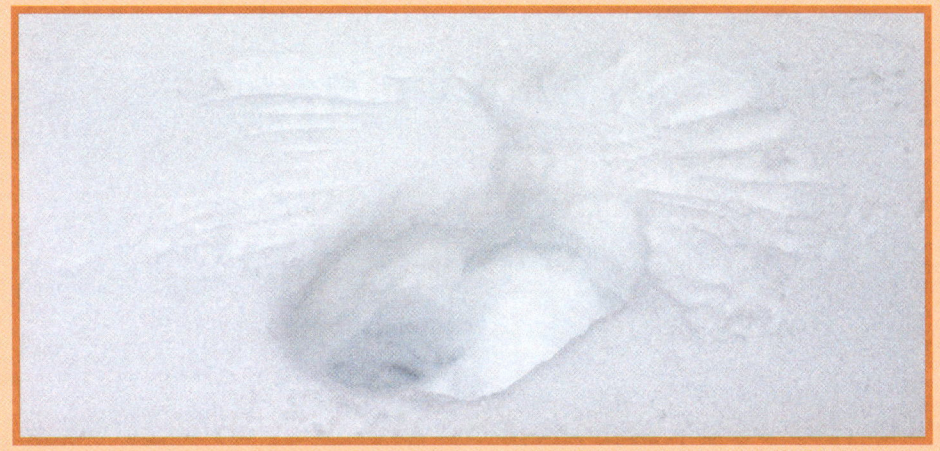
A print in the snow from a grouse bursting out.

Chapter 9

Yellow Warbler

Sweet-sweet-sweet-I-am-so-sweet.

This is the call of the yellow warbler. A warbler is a songbird. When a male warbler is trying to attract a female, it may sing over three thousand songs in one day!

The warbler migrates great distances. In the spring, it leaves South America or Central America. It flies all the way to Canada. It can be found in every province.

The warbler spends its summers in moist areas, such as the edge of swamps and streams and in gardens. It mainly eats insects, especially caterpillars, but sometimes it eats spiders and berries.

In June, the female yellow warbler builds a nest shaped like a deep cup. She lays three to six spotted eggs. The female sits on the nest, warming the eggs. The male brings her food.

But wait a minute! There's a large egg in the warblers' nest. What's that doing there?

It is a cowbird's egg. The cowbird often lays an egg in the nests of other birds, like warblers. It may even push one of the warbler's eggs out of the nest to make room!

Unlike other birds, if a female yellow warbler notices a cowbird's egg, she is not strong enough to push it out. Instead, if she has not laid her own egg, or has only laid one egg, she may build a new "floor" on her nest. She builds the floor to cover up the old eggs. She builds higher walls. She lays new eggs.

Sometimes the cowbird comes back again and lays another egg in this second storey of the nest. The female yellow warbler may once again add another new storey. Or she may leave the nest altogether and go and build a new one. Some nests have been found with six storeys!

Yellow warbler eggs hatch in ten to thirteen days. Now both parents busily feed the young. The young birds leave the nest after nine to twelve days. Their parents keep feeding them for another two to three weeks.

If a cowbird egg has hatched in the nest, the yellow warblers become foster parents. Often the cowbird hatches before the warblers. It grows quickly.

The cowbird is larger than the yellow warbler nestlings and it demands the most food. The warbler parents feed it more than their own babies.

Sometimes the cowbird is the only nestling to survive. You can see why mother warblers would want to cover up the cowbird eggs!

Chapter 10

Raven

Is that a raven? Or is that big, black bird a crow?

Ravens and crows look very similar, but ravens are larger than crows. In fact, they are the largest kind of songbird. Ravens have huge bills. They have long pointy feathers on their necks that make them look shaggy. Their tails are shaped like wedges or fans.

The raven is found across Canada, and is one of the most widespread birds in the world. It is also one of the most intelligent. It has adapted to live in many different habitats, from forests to deserts to mountains to plains to bogs.

Scientists say that ravens have among the largest brains of any bird. Ravens have learned to survive in difficult conditions. They can even work together to solve simple problems.

Ravens are also unusual because they like to play. They dangle upside-down from branches or telephone lines. They drop sticks and catch them. They have even been seen "tobogganing" down hills in winter!

Sometimes ravens steal golf balls from golf courses and hide them. Perhaps they think the small white balls are eggs!

But a raven can't play all of the time. It gets hungry. When it does, it eats . . . well, almost anything! It likes seeds, fruit, insects, molluscs, frogs, lizards and mice. It is a scavenger and will even eat roadkill. It also eats eggs and small birds.

A raven will also follow a pack of wolves or coyotes to a kill. When it finds one, it will alert other ravens and lead them to the food. Sharing this information helps the whole flock survive.

A raven doesn't only share news of a kill with other ravens. In the winter, if ravens find a carcass they will call other animals to come and feast. They wait until the predators have torn open the frozen body with their teeth and claws. Then the ravens can more easily help themselves to the meal that's left over.

Another clever way for a raven to find food is to wait for another bird, such as an eagle, to catch prey. As the eagle eats the prey, the raven bothers and nags at it until it flies away. The raven takes the remains for itself.

Most ravens mate for life, and they travel in pairs. As winter ends, they return to an old nest or build a new one. A male raven will bring some large sticks to a female, but she is the one that builds the nest. Some are as big as 1.5 metres wide.

Inside the large nest, the female builds a smaller cup-like nest with twigs. She lines it with mud, grass, fur, wool and sometimes trash.

The raven lays four to seven eggs. When the babies are born, they stay close to their parents for a little while, even after they leave the nest. They are protected by their parents. There is also much they can learn from them.

Soon they will join other young ravens in a flock. One day, when they are older, they will find mates of their own.